A
astronomy
AF481531

B
black ho

celestial

D
dark matter

exoplanet

F
formation

G
gravity

H
Hubble space telescope

interstellar

J
Jupiter

Kuiper Belt

light-year

M
Milky Way

N
nebula

O
Orion

P
planet

Q
quasar

R
radiation

S
solar

T
telescope

U
universe

V
Voyager

W
wormhole

X
Xenon

Y
year

Z
zodiac

9 798869 071668